AMMIE & SNOWBALL

A Senior Community's Adventure

with the Feral World

Jon Michael Miller

This story is based upon true events. However, names have been changed and the timeline compressed for the sake of more effective storytelling.

For my mother,

MARY ELLEN MILLER,

who taught me the love of Nature.

Special thanks to

Joyce Sacha for her recollection of the events and her photos of Ammie & kittens;

Kathy Lynch for her cover photo of Snowball;

and the Five O'clockers – Nancy Gummersall, Michael Downing, Nancy Grenier, Janet Milliard and Dorothy Williams – for their support.

Also, the members of the Dunedin Writers Group, Florida, for their wise counsel.

"What greater gift than the love of a cat."

Charles Dickens

AMMIE & SNOWBALL

One

I first saw the sorry-looking creature one morning on my way to my car in the parking lot of our condo building. The January day was chilly for Florida. Even in a flannel shirt I was shivering. The scrawny feline was traipsing among some ragged palmetto bushes along the edge of our covered parking where the lot ends at a patch of mulch and dried up hibiscus scrubs. Ribs evident, mostly gray with a white breast and a stub of tail, the sorry sight was on its way to somewhere. It looked sad, lonely, desperate. Of course, as a former literature major, I am aware of the fallacy of attributing human feelings to lesser beings, but as a caring mortal, I couldn't help but take immediate pity on the scraggily feline.

So I interrupted my trip to Walmart and went back to my second floor unit, opened a can of Fancy Feast that had been destined for our own two cats, went back outside and placed the tin dish along the path where I'd seen the stray, who was now on its journey out of sight. But I knew enough about the species to understand that their expeditions usually follow habitual routes lined with their various markings. Food in place, I went on to the giant discount store.

When I returned from my sock-buying errand – four pairs for ten bucks – I stopped by the dish and found most of the "Chicken Treat" gone. The remaining bits swarmed with ants. *This won't do*, thought I. So I conducted a visual search for a more ant-proof location.

I was also cognizant that felines operate on fairly regular schedules, at least my house cats do – Mojo and Isabel. So I figured if the gray, stubby-tailed stray did likewise and if I placed the food on the same path but a bit more onto the blacktop of the parking spaces at about the same time, I could avoid the nuisance of those voracious insects.

I might as well mention that we retirees sometimes have few enough causes and enough spare time to allow us to participate in such a project under the guise of being helpful to the world around us – you know, recycling, driving a neighbor to the podiatrist, and helping carry groceries in.

So next morning at about the same time, I ventured forth in my flannel shirt and placed the dish about two feet into the lot away from the cement curb. Then, to observe, I retreated to the second floor walkway in front of our unit.

Sure enough, there came the gray stray, skinny, wobbly, forlorn – until, that is, it spotted or got a whiff of the "Tuna Tenders." It paused, craned about, eventually swerved off its usual track and gorged. I felt swell. I'd done my good deed for the day. With this rosy inside feeling, I watched until the cat, licking its paws and cleaning its cheeks, turned and lay down in a pool of sunlight. That made me feel really fine, and I watched it the whole time it lay there, rolling around and grooming itself. Eventually, it got up and continued on its way.

I went inside and watched a rerun of *Seinfeld* until I realized I should probably go out and pick up the tin. When I got there, the dish was covered with ants carting off the bits of leftover tuna. *Something has to be done,* I thought. *My intention is not to feed ants. They are too far away from my species to engage my empathy.* I brushed the ones off that were still at their task, conducted another recon to discover an ant-proof location along the cat's daily route, and spotted a large patch of concrete out of the path of car traffic and far away enough from Mother Earth to be ant free.

At this point, however, my common sense told me that condo rules might discourage feeding wild animals. Certainly we don't want to feed rats, or mice, or opossums, for that matter, or even raccoons, which are kinda cute, or even squirrels, which are really cute, or armadillos which are not at all cute or, for heaven's sake, birds, which will poop all over our Subarus and Chevy pickups and walkways not to mention slow moving pedestrians using walkers or scooters.

Also, all that animal activity will bring coyotes that might try to feed on my neighbors' Chihuahuas, or even attract hawks which would attack gulls and bring us face to face with the horrors of predation and make us wonder about God's wisdom in having created a system based upon creatures forced to murder and consume one another in order to survive.

But I digress. Not feeding wildlife is a sensible restriction, I realized, except, perhaps, for sad and despairing felines. And now that I was thinking in broader terms, it occurred to me that I might gain this particular forlorn creature's trust, befriend it and find it a home where it could spend the remainder if its days in comfort and love.

Not in *our* home, though, already with its maximum pet capacity, but in someone's. Of course, such a project might take some time, and in the meantime a fussy neighbor might object to the rule violation, but I vaguely recalled Ronald Reagan's edict to "act now and apologize later."

Thus, despite the many risks, I vowed to save this cat from its fraught existence in the vicious wilds of nature.

Jon Michael Miller

Two

From my numerous trips to Jamaica I was aware of the patois proverb: *Try feed a mada dawg, 'im turn 'round bite you.* Those wise words extend far beyond feeding needy animals. They warn us, in general, of the risk incurred in helping others: "Try help a needy neighbor, they rob you of your hard earned money." "Give millions to a desperate nation, the funds go into the pockets of oligarchs." There are numerous applications to this bit of island wisdom about a *mada dawg.* To emphasize the proverb's sagacity, I'll repeat it: *Try feed a mada dawg, 'im turn 'round bite you.*

But we should help others, shouldn't we? – especially the down and out. To keep ourselves safe, we might do our duty simply by contributing to the Salvation Army and the Red Cross, thus aiding the victims of life's cruelties in the abstract, and keeping risky involvements from invading our personal comforts. But – and not for the first time I must admit – my heartstrings were pulling at me regarding the real, actual, presence of this distressed kitty.

Hence, the gray cat and I formed a relationship, not face to face, but each morning, I placed a dish of Beefy Brisket or Turkey Tenders in the ant-free spot. And after I retreated, the cat crept out of the underbrush and gulped its breakfast down.

Then, in about a week something changed in our association. One day, I noticed the cat lingering in the ragged holly-compacta hedge, clearly, it seemed, waiting for me.

"Oh, how nice," I thought. "I'll nurture our friendship until I can find it a home." I placed the dish on the concrete and lingered, hoping the creature would emerge from the bushes. Finally, I realized, it preferred to dine in private, so I withdrew to the vantage point of the second story catwalk. Then it came out, ate its fill, luxuriated in the sunlight and moved on.

I called around to animal adoption centers to see if there was a place I could take this forlorn feral, have it spayed, and either find an adoptee or, at the very least, release it back into the wild where it would not propagate its kind. There are such places, I discovered. I didn't want to take it to the county animal services or even leave it in the dead of night at the SPCA center for chances they would, as can be nicely said, "put it down." The "catch-neuter-return" services charged a donation but were even willing to come to your place and trap the wayward creature. But my real plan was to find it a loving home, albeit, not mine.

This plan brought my neighbors into play. "Who among them," I wondered, "might like to save a miserable being from a cruel and perilous existence?"

Nan came immediately to mind. To understand this narrative, you need to know about Nan. The following account will involve some intricate and idiosyncratic details of my condo life, so try to stay awake. I reside in an over-55 condo community begun 1970 with the building I live in, and expanding through the years to sixteen buildings in all. It is neither gated nor posh. My building, the Amherst, has four wings that meet in a common hub where there are lobbies, mailboxes, a laundry room, an elevator, a trash room, a storage room — you get the picture if you haven't dozed off.

My wing – the D wing – faces across the parking lot and some struggling shrubbery to the A wing, each with three stories, eight units apiece – nothing a bit fancy, common catwalks, same deep maroon doors and white window treatments. The parking lot has some covered parking, but most of us just park in the weather. None of the units has a balcony in back. Though the community is not gated, it's pretty safe.

With that vital background, let's get back to Nan. My wife Yukika (she's Japanese) and I have lived here now about fifteen years. You already know I have two cats. I'm a retired college teacher, now using much of my time to write self-published novels. After a few years in residence, I decided to enjoy my Florida existence by taking an hour or two late in the afternoon when the sun is far enough west of Amherst Building to provide shade on the catwalk in front of my unit. Due to fire regulations, chairs permanently occupying the walkway are illegal, so I take a folding lawn chair out and in, as needed.

Though it might not sound it, relaxing in a public area has its pitfalls, particularly regarding privacy. Here is a rule of life, in case you don't already know it. If you occupy the same space, every day at the same time, others will begin to show up like iron shards to a magnet. If you don't quite accept this generalization as truth, you can conduct an experiment and you'll see its accuracy. It has nothing to do with how you look, your personality, your intentions – well, just try it, you'll see. In my case, the first person to appear was Nan.

When she first sidled up to me, she was in her mid-eighties, a nicely dressed woman, short gray hair, slightly bent over walk, orthopedic sneakers and a combo grocery bag/pocketbook. And, kind eyes. She lives in the opposite wing, second floor, as I, directly across from me. She must have seen me sitting out there reading and eventually thought I might need some company, so on her way to the mailboxes each day about five o'clock, she treaded down the walkway to say hello and chat a little.

Like most condo conversations, ours started with the weather, how long we lived in Florida – her twenty years, me twelve – what we'd done in our professions – she a dental hygienist, I a college teacher – back to the weather – usually the same but with some minor variations that could be noted, such as, "The breeze is picking up," or "The clouds are thicker – maybe we'll get some rain."

Nan, in particular, was fascinated by planes crossing over as if they were spectacular new inventions, rarely seen. "Ah," she'd say, interrupting whatever the theme of our conversation happened to be, "look at that! How beautiful!" This would happen two or three times every time we talked, our community being on the direct flight path of Allegiant Airlines. Widowed several times, and divorced several others, she now lived alone.

As far as our daily meetings went, human contact was the idea – not in-depth discussion. It became a habit, Nan and I, so regular that I felt guilty her standing there, me sitting – so, I drove out to Walmart and bought another chair, which I set up every day beside mine, so I needn't feel like a cad. Our association became a daily ritual, so much so that if, for some reason, I wasn't able to make it that day, I felt obligated to call her and let her know.

Verifying the law of people gathering (as if it needs verification), eventually others showed up. Third to the group was Jan – my next door neighbor usually in flamboyantly designed Zumba attire, also widowed several times with a large family in the area who often dropped by to visit. Then came Mitch, who lived two doors down, drove a Mercedes and had stories about every car he'd ever owned including a peddle-Cadillac his dad gave him on his fourth birthday. Always accompanying Mitch was Dolly, his part-Pomeranian, who became the star of the show, so to speak, receiving treats from all.

Then Dorothy added her presence, a very organized, common-sense woman who listened more than spoke, but had a reservoir of anecdotes, if pressed. Finally, Pam from the first floor joined in – a country sort with country grammar and a genuine concern for everyone's health.

I went back to Walmart and bought another chair for her because I noticed she was uncomfortable standing and she had to walk up a full flight of stairs to join us. To the other residents of Amherst Building, we became known as the Five O'clock Club, often attracting temporary attendees who happened to be out and about with their Shi Tzus and Jack Russells and who couldn't resist a gathering – those iron shards again. So much for my finishing up with *War and Peace*. Oh, and I might add one of the funny features of the group – Nan, Jan, & Pam.

Thus was the social milieu into which the feral cat entered the picture. Well, not right away. For a week or so, I merely dropped off a tin dish of Chicken Pate at the ant-free location and withdrew, returning an hour or so later to pick up the wiped-clean container and feeling a nice little surge of pleasure from having done something useful for a fellow creature.

Three

The tale takes a turn, however. One day when I went to drop off the morning meal, I discovered, to my surprise, another dish of food already there. It was one of those separated dishes, with half dry food and half wet, along with a dish of water. I stopped in my tracks and looked around for a sign of another human presence – none. Hmm – competition. Or, perhaps, cooperation.

When I went back to remove my empty tin, the others still remained, giving me the impression of a permanent presence. Dishes there permanently would not be good. They would attract other animals, among them possible other ferals, and might start a community of cats, cats everywhere, nesting under parked vehicles and exciting controversy.

Out of curiosity, I visited the site after the 5-O'clock Group had disbanded and found a newly loaded dish of food. I supposed that eventually the new donor and I would cross paths and could coordinate both our process and our philosophies.

My supposition proved correct. The very next morning I ran into her, both of us having arrived at the same time.

"Good morning," I said. "I was wondering who was helping out."

"Hello," she said, a fully loaded double-dish in her hand and a small, chubby white poodle at her feet.

"I'm Mike," I said.

"Jocelyn. And this is Lulu. She's blind."

Short, bordering on stocky, Jocelyn was a fullback of a woman with cropped blond hair, a round face and bright blue eyes. I knew her as a recent arrival who parked her white Kia Soul near the wing's end staircase and who lived on the first floor next to Pam.

"Have you seen the recipient of our efforts?" I asked.

"You mean the stray? Yes, poor thing."

Still holding my loaded dish, hers already on the ground, I said, "I think we should be careful about leaving our dishes out all the time. It will most likely bring other varmints – rats and such."

"Oh, you might be right about that."

"It'll upset the other residents."

"Well, screw them."

"But they'll take it to the Board, and the Board will...."

"Screw the Board."

"Well, they'll issue fines."

"Fines?"

"Yeah, we're kinda breaking the rules."

"I always figure rules are meant to be broken."

"Look, Jocelyn, why don't we make a plan. I want to win this cat's trust and try to get her spayed and find her a home. It'll take some time, but during the process we don't want to create a feral community here, don't you agree?"

"Well, I suppose so."

"So we can work together," I added. "I'll take the morning shift and you take the evening. But we can't leave the dishes here all the time. Just on her schedule. I give her about an hour, then pick up the dish. And she might not trust us with your dog."

"Lulu? Oh, she's old and blind, completely harmless."

I leaned down and petted Lulu. Looking up at Jocelyn, I said, "It's good of you to take care of her."

"I'd never put her down, if that's what you're thinking."

"I didn't mean that. But some people might, you know."

"Not me."

I rose. "Well, what do you think of my strategy?"

"Makes sense, I guess. You might be right. I like animals but not rats."

"Good. I have two cats inside, so I'll take this food back, but tomorrow morning I'll take care of this, and you do it in the evenings, but don't leave the dish out long, okay? And if you back off with Lulu, the cat might come to trust us."

"Lulu won't hurt anyone."

"But the cat doesn't know that. And our mission is to find her a home, not to create a permanent thing here, right?"

"I guess so. You seem kinda hung up on rules."

"Nice meeting you, Jocelyn."

"Nice meeting you too, I guess."

Thus, I retreated with my loaded dish, unsure about where this would go.

The strategy to make friends with this wild creature (the cat, not Jocelyn) seemed to be working. Each morning about six, I took out the food and saw the cat, now fattening up, hiding in the Indian goose grass that grew wild at that end of the parking lot. She waited until I was well gone, but from my view in front of my unit I watched her eat and loll about in the early sunlight.

There was a bench nearby where people went to smoke, and I wondered what would happen if I began sitting there motionless as the feline munched down the Ocean-fish Delight. Next morning I gave my plan a try. I set down the dish and settled on the bench about ten yards away.

For a while the cat eyed me and stayed in the brush. But apparently the food was too powerful a lure, and after about twenty minutes, she slinked into the open, eyes on me, and began eating. She constantly peered up to see if I posed a threat. I looked the other way as if I were observing a couple of crows perched on the telephone wires. When I looked back, she was eating, but after she was finished she decided to bask elsewhere. Looking back now and then, she ventured across the overgrown lawn toward the Bank of America, carefully on the lookout for enemies.

This kitty was not interested in human contact. I retrieved the dish and went inside, deciding to adopt the new tactic until she recognized me as unthreatening. But it struck me how awful it would be to live in her world, ever scared, ever watching out for danger, ever on guard. How well humans have evolved to live in relative safety from nature, except, of course, from each other!

Four

Then I noticed a change in Jocelyn's approach to the situation. Instead of placing the food in the area I'd chosen, she started using the concrete between her Kia Soul and Bill Kreider's ancient Dodge van that had a seriously rusting roof about to label itself an "eyesore" as per the condo's rules and regs.

Now, Jocelyn left the dish approximately thirty steps from her front door at the end of our wing. And she started sing-songing out to the recipient of her benevolence: "Kitty, Kitty. Here you are, Kitty, Kitty. Here's your food, here's your sup-sup. Come and get it, little girl." Then she went inside and watched from behind her screen door.

It took a few days for the cat to respond to these inviting kitty tunes. The lure of the food, however, eventually wore down her caution. But if someone happened to walk by on the way to the nearby Publix, or walking their dog, she made a mad rush to under the car or the van. I expected a few neighbors to be up in arms about Jocelyn's approach, but apparently most of them shared her attitude toward rules and regulations as announced in the condominium bylaws, namely, the belief that rules are made to be broken. I, however, intended to break the rules more subtly and continued my morning tactic further away from the building.

As the evening mealtime eventually worked out, though, Jocelyn's feeding time occurred shortly after she arrived home from the real estate office where she worked – just after five. That timing meant that the kitty appeared during the Five O'clock Club's congregation on the second floor walkway. And the cat's arrival to Jocelyn's siren song became the central focus of the gathering, which badly needed a central focus. All eyes turned first toward Jocelyn's voice and then to the emergence of the feral from the boxwood hedge.

"Ammie," someone said. "We'll call her Ammie."

"Ammie? Why Ammie?"

"Short for Amherst, our building."

"Why not just Amherst?"

"Ammie is much better for a cat than Amherst."

"Why?"

"I don't know. Just the sound of it. 'Amherst' sounds like some stuffy college professor delivering a sermon."

"A lecture, maybe," someone alertly said. "Preachers deliver sermons, not professors."

But with that important correction made, the cat's name nevertheless stuck – *Ammie*, the star of the afternoon show. And in the mornings of my private show, the cat looked healthier and healthier as the days went along. Then, however, her appearance became a little more than merely healthy. She began to bulge in the middle. Rumors began.

"Look at that," someone noted. "She must be pregnant."

Finally, a week later, there could be no doubt.

"Where does she live?" someone asked.

Everyone looked at me.

"I don't know where she lives," I answered.

"Didn't you ever follow her?"

"No. Why would I do that?"

"To see where she lives."

"What does it matter where she lives?" I said. "Maybe she lives over toward the bank."

"What makes you think that?"

"After she eats, she goes over that way."

"Well, she's obviously with child," someone noted.

"Yes, and that means soon there will be little Ammies all over the place."

"Oh, that will be so cute."

"It will be a big problem. Because in a while those little Ammies will have their own little Ammies. Then what?"

"That's not our problem. They'll be over there toward the bank, like Mike says."

"She'll eventually bring them here – to the food."

"That's true," someone agreed.

"Then what?" someone else piped up.

"We'll find them homes," I said. "Nan, you live all alone. Wouldn't you like to have a kitten?"

"I would love to, but I'm allergic to cats."

"I'd rather have a dog than a cat," said Jan.

"I can't have a cat," Pam said. "Ever since my pug passed away, I decided no more pets. It's just too sad."

"Like you," Mr. Mike," added Dorothy, "I already have two cats."

"I have Dolly," Mitch said, referring to his Pomeranian.

"Maybe Jocelyn will take one."

"She has Lulu."

"My goal," I reminded everyone, "is to catch Ammie, have her spayed, and then this whole issue is moot."

"Moot?" Jan said. "What's *moot* mean? I always wondered."

"Irrelevant," Mitch said. "A legal term."

"What do you mean my question is irrelevant?"

"Not your question," Mitch said. "The meaning of the word *moot. Moot* means irrelevant."

"Who came up with that?" Jan answered. "Who do these lawyers think they are anyways?"

"Well," Pam said, "the point ain't moot in the present case, at least. Ammie is fatter than a cow."

And it was true that the cat's bulging belly probably indicated more than her now-steady diet. Her midriff almost dragged on the ground.

Then, one day, she didn't arrive in the morning, or in the evening.

"She must have had them," someone at the gathering said.

Jocelyn was out and about, carrying the food dish and crooning her kitty song. But still no Ammie. Jocelyn wandered up and down the grounds to no avail.

"Maybe something happened to her," someone suggested.

"A coyote, maybe," someone else said.

"Or a truck out on 54th Avenue."

"They come by here so fast," another voice.

"Most likely feeding her babies," Mitch said wisely.

Five

After three long days, Ammie showed up in the morning. I'd been keeping up my feeding ventures, waiting, then taking the food back in to my own cats. But here she was again, looking thin, haggard and hungry as a pig. I went in and brought her another dish, and she didn't even bother to run and hide from me. After eating ravenously, she trotted immediately away toward the bank.

This time, I followed at a distance. She went across a ragged lawn, down into a drainage ditch and up the other side, across the pavement of the bank's drive-thru lane, through the bank's parking lot and down into another drainage ditch, toward 54th where the ditch ended at a culvert. At the cement structure with three iron, prison-like bars, she squeezed through into the dark interior.

One mystery solved.

That afternoon she showed up between the Kia and the Dodge van for Jocelyn's feast. Everyone up on the second floor near my door oohed and ahhed at the now-mommy cat's reappearance. Jocelyn seemed jubilant at the kitty's return, scaring the skin and bones creature to under her car. Jocelyn had to back off. She stood at her screen door, unable to keep her feet still.

As for the exact location of Ammie's lair, I was mum on the subject. I didn't want anyone, especially Jocelyn, to go over there and bother the new mother, who was busy enough. So the normal morning and evening feeding routine resumed, and Ammie gradually regained her normal weight.

Then one morning before I went out to deliver the cat's breakfast, I heard pounding on my door. It was Jocelyn.

"I have a problem, Mike," she said, rubbing her fists together.

"What is it, Jocelyn?"

"Ammie won't let me near my car."

"What? What's that?"

"She hisses and charges at me every time I get near the car. And I have to get to work."

"Why would she do that?"

"Maybe she brought her kittens here, and they're under the car."

"Did you look?"

"I'm not dressed very well to get down on my hands and knees."

"I'll be right down," I said.

"Well, hurry up. I'm in the dog house bad enough at work."

At the Kia Soul, I saw an angry, protective Ammie peering out from around the driver's-side front tire. I managed to get a glimpse underneath, well enough to determine there was not a litter of kittens clustered on the pavement.

"Oh, my God!" Jocelyn said. "Maybe they're inside the motor."

"I highly doubt that," I answered. "The actual motor is pretty well covered."

"It happened to my friend up in New Port Ritchie. A cat had her kittens in the motor, or whatever you wanna call it."

"What did your friend do?"

"Called the fire department. I don't remember the details. But I gotta get to work."

"How 'bout I drive you. Then I'll try to figure out what's happening. You can call me when you're ready to come home, and I'll come get you."

"You'll do that?"

"Sure. We're neighbors."

After I took her downtown to her job, I returned to find Ammie still vehemently guarding Jocelyn's Soul. Close to five o'clock,

Jocelyn called me; I set out the chairs for the Club and drove downtown to pick her up.

"What happened?" she asked eagerly.

"No change."

"She's still under there?"

"Indeed she is."

"She must have the kittens in the motor."

"Well, up under there somewhere. There's plenty of nooks and crannies."

"But why would she...?"

"They're probably getting too big to suckle, so she brought them close to the food."

"Did you see them? Hear them?"

"No. But why else would she be guarding that territory so fiercely?"

When we returned, the Five O'clock Club was in full swing. They noticed me bringing Jocelyn in. I trembled a bit at what they might have been supposing. When I got out of my Elantra, I shouted out my explanation: "She might have her kittens under there."

"We know," yelled Mitch. "That wild thing almost attacked Dolly when we walked past."

Jocelyn bent down to have a look under her Soul. Ammie hissed terribly.

"I guess we should pop the hood," I said, "and have a look."

"Uh, okay, I guess so. Should we call the fire department?"

"Let's check it out first."

The Five O'clock members had now sidled down the walkway to just above us. I went to the passenger side to distract Ammie and allow Jocelyn to slip into the driver's side and pop the hood. That accomplished, I reached under, loosened the latch and slowly lifted.

There, just behind the air-cleaner cover were four little kitten faces, side by side, big eyes staring right at me. I backed up in surprise, looked up at the group and waved four fingers. Quietly, I lowered the hood again.

Everyone was stirred up, fidgeting but trying to stay quiet as per the index finger I placed in front of my lips to indicate silence. I backed off and looked at Jocelyn who was quaking.

"Do you have a cardboard box, or a pet carrier?" I asked.

"Yes, a carrier for Lulu."

"Go get it. I'm going upstairs to get some gloves. I'll try to grab these critters and then we'll figure out what to do with them."

I bounded up the stairs ... well, ran up ... well, actually kind of rapidly hobbled. The Five O'clockers cleared the way for me to get to my place. I grabbed the gloves and went back to the Kia where Jocelyn waited with the carrier. Again I lifted the hood. The four little faces stared back. One by one I deftly lifted three of them and put them into the carrier. Two were black, one was all gray, but the fourth one had managed to get down into the interior of the car's underpinnings.

The three safely contained, the mom hissing like crazy, I began the search for the remaining kitten. By this time, a couple who lived next to Jocelyn, Katy and Don, came out to see what the ruckus was all about. After being informed by numerous versions of the situation, this couple, familiar with the wilderness, often vacationing in the mountains near Ashville, North Carolina, swung into action, poking around the engine mounting from above and around the wheel wells and finally on their backs from below. Poor Ammie had now retreated in a fury to under the Dodge van.

At last the kitten was at least located, but it had wedged its way into a space that made it irretrievable except by possibly stink-bombing it out. The attempt to capture it went on well after sunset and was finally given up.

"We'll let things develop," Don said. "Don't worry, we'll get the clever rascal. We'll see what happens with the light of day."

"But how will I get to work?" Jocelyn queried.

I volunteered to drive her until we managed to capture the fourth kitten.

In the meantime I had possession of three kits in a carrier. They were too young to be left on their own, and the SPCA and Animal Services were closed, so I called an emergency pet hospital and was told that they would take the kittens and rehab them until they were ready for adoption.

"We don't want them put down," I said.

"Oh, no. We have this issue all the time. There's a woman who will hand-feed them until they can eat on their own. Then she'll find them homes."

"Marvelous. I'll bring them right there."

Before I left, however, a number of neighbors wanted to see them and take pictures through the opened top of the carrier, after which I drove them to the pet hospital and bid them farewell, assured that they'd be well taken care of.

Next morning, at the standard feeding area, the situation regarding the fourth kitten clarified. It was now in the weeds near her momma as the latter crept out to eat, looking wildly around constantly. I had backed well off. Without making a sound, the kitten stayed mostly hidden, waiting for Ammie to return.

At least we now knew the baby was safe and sound and wouldn't be ground up by firing pistons, Jocelyn's imagined fear, even though firing pistons were hardly in play. Thankful for this stroke of good fortune, Jocelyn was able to drive herself to work, and I was left with the problem of how, now, to proceed.

Jon Michael Miller

Six

By this time, it had become clear that we needed to find the momma a home. Either that, or plan to support a colony of feral cats. This creature, despite the challenges posed by its perilous existence, was well aware of her mission on this earth – to procreate her kind. It didn't apparently occur to her that she might become someone's "pet," to be hugged, cuddled, and played with in a warm, safe environment.

For a few days she wandered about the parked cars, meowing and searching for her lost kids. She struck us Five-O'clockers as sad and desperate. We could all sympathize with her plight. But after a few days she seemed to have accepted the situation and focused on the one offspring remaining, an adorable white and gray spotted little thing, with a dab of gray on its nose as if it had pressed against some dust.

Thinking the baby should have a name, Katy suggested *Snowball,* readily accepted by everyone. It wasn't too long before the youngster was grown enough to be following Ammie to the food dish.

Now I was left with the problem of how to find them both homes. Realizing we had to catch them somehow, I called Animal Services, but they would come for them only if they were in containers – the officials wouldn't come to trap them though they referred me to someone who would.

This person, however, was not interested in only two cats. Working for donations, he preferred larger catches. Nor could he guarantee they would be returned to us neutered and vaccinated. He told me to go to Home Depot and buy a trap. Then I could take them to a vet who would do the surgery and release them back to me. Snowball, however, was still too young for the operation.

In the meantime, the momma and child were the hit of the Five O'clockers' gatherings. Jocelyn arrived home every day about that time, came out crooning her kitty song and put the food down. We watched the momma/daughter from the second floor as they nourished themselves.

Although they'd begun trusting the area, they were not at all accessible to human contact. As a week or so went by, however, accessibility began to change for the kitten. No longer suckling, but instead relying entirely on the food Jocelyn and I supplied, the young one became less cautious. Momma was no longer as strict.

I sat closer to the food dish, especially in the evening when it was nearer our building between the Soul and the Dodge van. I asked around for someone to take the kitten once

our mission to rob it of its reproductive pow-
ers was accomplished. Everyone had an ex-
cuse. It amazed me how many people are allergic to cats.

At Home Depot I purchased a me-
dium-sized animal trap for $24.99 plus tax. I
spent several hours trying to figure how the
damn thing worked. It was a rectangular cage
with a lift-up door on one end and a plate toward the back, beyond which food was placed
as bait. You fastened the front door up and
open. It was attached it to a rod that con-
nected to the plate. The victim would enter,
step on the metal floor-plate to get to the
food and – WHAM – the front door would
snap shut, rather violently, and the creature
was contained.

Waiting for Snowball to come of age
for surgery, I sat ever closer, inch by inch, to
the food area, with a feather toy and a little
bell attached to a stick which I jiggled about

as the kitten pranced around trying to subdue it, following its irrepressible instinct to capture prey. The mom was not at all interested in fun and games as she sat near the van washing. There was no getting near her whatsoever. Move too close and you received a horrific, bare-fanged hiss accompanied by a ferocious growl. That hiss frightened even passing, leashed canines four times Ammie's size.

But Snowball was vulnerable to her own unsuspecting innocence. And it was clear that Jocelyn was bonding to her even though she wouldn't be able to take her because of her blind poodle. Nevertheless, she crooned to the kitten, explained her job problems and teased her with the feathery toy. And we all giggled from the walkway above. In my own time I rehearsed with the trap, waiting for the opportunity to fulfill my duty of removing these creatures from their purpose as God had dictated. As a lit buff, I was not unaware of my interference with the way nature intended – not that different from Captain Ahab's purpose with the Great White Whale. From that literary masterpiece I should have learned the dangers of pitting oneself against the natural world.

Anyway, days were turning into weeks, and Snowball was becoming more and more trustful until one evening as I teased her with the toy, bringing her ever closer to the tips of my sneakers, I realized I might just be able to reach down and snatch her. Her attention was entirely on subduing the bird-like distraction. A nervous heat rose through me – it was that primal moment when the deer moves unaware into the crosshairs of one's rifle and the decisive instant is upon you.

Just lean down and grab her, a voice in my head whispered. *Now is the moment.*

And so I did – just bent down and grabbed her. Oh, and what a shriek! And what a shriek from momma. And a few yelps of surprise from the Five O'clockers. But I had the small, wriggling creature in my grasp, now clutched close to my breastbone.

"Get the carrier," I barked to Jocelyn. "Quick."

Momma cat was furious, pacing in front of the Dodge, tempted but holding back from attacking the kidnapper, i.e., me. Snowball wriggled and cried out as I clutched her to my chest. Jocelyn came out with the carrier, and I quickly shoved Snowball in and latched the door. Success! – Followed by pulsing waves of guilt. Followed by a pulsing rationalization to justify my act. *This is best. She will get a safe, happy home.*

"You did the right thing," my fellow Five O'clockers assured me.

But I didn't feel the certainty of that.

Jon Michael Miller

Seven

The day of Snowball's capture was a Sunday. Having done some research, I found out that the trappers who took their captive ferals for surgery used the SPCA vet services on 31st Street, closed Sundays, of course. So I had Snowball in a carrier. When I took the carrier into my unit, my other two cats went a little wild, telling me this was not the place to keep little, terrified Snowball. Katy and Don agreed to keep her at their place until I could take her to the SPCA first thing Monday morning. Ammie was still wandering around searching for her kidnapped kid.

With the carrier in the trunk, I arrived at the SPCA twenty minutes before it opened, sitting with the towel-covered carrier. Cats usually don't fear what they cannot see. Snowball was silent as I whispered gently to her.

When they finally opened up, I soon learned that they did not take animals without an appointment, and they were booked until Wednesday. Don and Katy agreed to take care of her. They let her race around their apartment destroying things.

In the meantime the Five O'clockers donated to the cost of the medical service, each contributing twenty bucks for the $120 cost. Finally, early Wednesday morning I returned to the medical facility and was told I could pick up the patient that afternoon, which I did. She'd been given a regimen of shots, de-fleaed and spayed. Quieted by the anesthesia, she was silent on the ride back. Once again, Katy and Don kept her until next morning when we let her outside again, free to join her mom.

The reunion was stirring as they smelled and licked each other. Now the search to find Snowball a home began, but at least we were all comforted by her not eventually contributing to a feral cat community.

As the daily feeding continued, Jocelyn became bolder about keeping the two cats closer to her front door. Ammie had clearly claimed that area as her territory. Snowball soon seemed to forget her nearly one week terror and started playing with the feather toy again. Jocelyn spread some catnip around, causing our laughter as the two cats rolled in it and got stoned.

But no one was available to take on the responsibility of ownership. I stuck to the cats' morning feedings at the more distant spot, but Jocelyn crooned her song, luring them ever closer to her unit.

Then one morning about a week later, Snowball did not show up for her morning meal. Ammie did, but no Snowball. I thought maybe she'd got hold of a sparrow for her breakfast, but then she didn't turn up for the evening feeding at Jocelyn's. Jocelyn wandered around the grounds calling out for her, holding a dish of food, searching in the shrubbery, in the stairwells, along the walkways, and through the parking areas. But no Snowball. At the end of her search, Jocelyn was in tears.

"Where could she be?" she cried. "What happened to her?"

"A coyote, maybe," someone said, which set Jocelyn off into a new wave of tears.

"Maybe hit by a car."

Jocelyn hurried out to 54th Avenue to see if Snowball's lifeless body lay squashed in the middle of the busy street, but no.

"I guess she just wandered off," someone suggested," to find her own territory. Cats are territorial, you know."

For the next few days, we all searched, especially Jocelyn.

But Snowball had gone, whether to her demise by a predator or by accident, or just to some other place. A week went by, and after all the searching and the hypothetical musing, we had to face the tragic fact. We had lost our communally adopted, gray and white, dusty-nosed darling.

Jon Michael Miller

Eight

Word of the heartbreak spread throughout Amherst Building, and about a week later, a Sunday afternoon as I was watching the Master's Tournament, I heard a loud knock on my door. It was Jocelyn, wringing her hands, pacing nervously. I opened up.

"I think I found her," she said, her cheeks wet with tears.

I stepped outside. "Where?" I asked.

"Well, you know Judy, don't you? The lady with that cute Jack Russel up in 306?"

"Sure, the redhead with a wisecrack for every occasion."

"Well, she just came over to my place. She was riding up on the elevator with Carlos, and guess what?"

"Go on," I said.

"He told Judy he had a new kitten and that he caught it on our stairwell at two-thirty in the morning when he was coming in. Probably from that crack house across the street. He said the kitten bit him, but that he took it home anyway. Then Judy told him that the kitten had been spayed, and he said, 'Good, that'll save me a hundred and fifty bucks.' She came right over to tell me, and I went up there and knocked on Carlos's door, but he didn't answer."

I must now interrupt the flow of the narrative to familiarize you with Carlos. Though almost all of our residents are over fifty-five, Carlos, probably in his mid-thirties, lives there in his father's place. He seldom works, no driver license, just hangs around, smoking, with a lot of five-minute visitors, mostly young males. He congregates across the street at a place once televised in an episode of "Cops."

Jocelyn was weeping, rubbing her cheeks with her fist.

I took a breath. "Well, at least she's alive."

"Yes, and I want her back. I don't trust that hoodlum with her."

"We need to call the police," I said. "We shouldn't take it on ourselves to mess with Carlos."

And call the police, I did. While we waited for the deputy sheriff to arrive, word had mysteriously spread among the neighbors. Half a dozen or so had gathered in front of Jocelyn's first floor unit. Soon a cruiser rolled in to the parking lot. A small woman, wearing a belt loaded with devices, got out of the car, strolled over and listened to the stories coming at her from various impassioned speakers. She jotted notes on a small pad.

"Now just relax," she said at last. "Who does the kitten belong to?"

"Technically she belongs to me," I said, "because I had to register her at the vet. We're trying to...."

"She's mine!" Jocelyn shouted.

"Yes," I readily agreed. "Right."

"This derelict man upstairs stole her," Jocelyn said, red-faced. "I want her back. I went up there, but he won't answer his door."

"How do you know he's at home?" the cop asked.

"I heard something in there."

"He's a big guy, rough," I added. "Been arrested several times."

"All right," the deputy said. "I'll go there and check."

"I'm coming along," Jocelyn said.

"All right, but we don't need a crowd. You others wait here."

Nine

So we waited, all rejoicing that we hadn't lost Snowball after all. No coyotes, no car accident, no wandering off to new territories. She was still here, with us. It was like a resurrection. Some marveled that God had intervened.

After ten minutes or so, Jocelyn came trotting from the lobby, shedding tears and clutching little Snowball to her chest. We were all thrilled, some tears flowing among us also. The deputy followed.

We gathered around, each giving terrified Snowball pats on her little head.

"The fellow," the deputy said, "didn't open when I knocked. Then this lady called, 'Kitty, Kitty,' and I heard a tiny meow. When the fellow finally opened up, I went inside but couldn't find the kitten. Then I heard the meow in answer to this lady here, and it seemed like the sound was coming from an end table by the sofa. And when I opened the drawer, there was the kitten. A happy ending, I guess. Now who is the proper owner?"

"I am," Jocelyn repeated with authority.

"But this man here said the kitten was his." The deputy looked toward me.

"Just because I took her to the vet, but I'll sign it over to Jocelyn. They gave me the forms, in case we found Snowball a home."

"Well," the deputy said, "I guess you just found her one."

After that fateful and happy day, Jocelyn began the process of taking Snowball in. For a while the young cat spent most of her time outdoors, roaming around, climbing trees, chasing birds and exploring the roofs of the covered parking. Now and then one of us found footprints on our windshield, but more and more she was lured into the interior of Jocelyn's domain, even with a blind poodle about.

Jon Michael Miller

Ten

Ammie, however, was another story. For a month or so, she and Snowball hung out together, and Jocelyn and I maintained our feeding strategy. In the mornings I found Ammie waiting for me, and the Five O'clockers still observed the evening feasting. Then a visitor showed up — a healthy-looking black male with evil eyes.

I soon realized I was characterizing the male visitor as a dad might see a bad-boy teen trying to date his virgin daughter. Of course the feline prowler was only following its instincts as Nature intended.

At first, Ammie didn't like him — spat and growled — but then one afternoon we saw them lolling in the sunshine together. The necessity of trapping Ammie weighed ever heavier on my mind.

A few people began to complain to the board. The owner of the van, who travelled a lot for his job and was seldom in residence, was furious to find footprints on the hood as though without the footprints his van was not a rusted-out monstrosity. He got into a shouting match with Jocelyn, and no one defeats Jocelyn in mouth to mouth combat.

"I'm gonna poison that f-ing cat," he said.

"You do that, and your wreck of a vehicle will go up in flames."

Another fellow, bulky, bearded, who rode his bicycle around the neighborhood most of the day, threatened to shoot Ammie.

"I hate cats," he said. "They're a scourge."

I was surprised he knew the word *scourge*. But human beings are full of surprises.

He redoubled his threat by voicing it at an official association meeting. Ammie –

and by extension, I – seemed to have ignited a civil war among the retirees.

Of course, merely spaying Ammie and releasing her into her now-not-very-wild world would solve only part of the problem. And due to the intruder with the evil eyes – the eyes of raw seduction for his own lecherous pleasure only – I realized that the proverbial clock was ticking.

So while there was still time, I practiced with the trap. Ammie was not one whit closer to being touched, let alone picked up. After I'd thoroughly familiarized myself with the simple mechanism, I felt ready to go into action. I'd read on the internet that spaying could take place even during pregnancy, a relief because after all Ammie's cavorting about in the sunshine with the horny intruder, now dubbed "Tux" because of his all black body except for his white chest, it was obvious to everyone who the father of that first litter was.

Finally, at the morning feeding time, I set the trap and put it out. I even made an appointment at the SPCA for the surgery and timed the capture so that I wouldn't have to keep Ammie penned up several days as had happened with Snowball. But at the moment of truth, I received quite a surprise.

I placed the food dish at the back of the cage, just beyond the metal plate that would spring the trap. And after the intended victim carefully checked out this new thing, circling several times, craning her head at the opening, sniffing the air, withdrawing and venturing back by her hunger and the scent of Salmon Celebration, she tiptoed in. Warily, so warily, she moved toward the metal plate, eventually stepped onto it, and as I watched with eager anticipation, she ate the bowl clean. Then, still standing on the metal plate, she blithely washed a bit, turned around and exited, safe and sound. She stretched out nearby in the sun and washed.

When she finally wandered off, I found a strong little twig and pressed it against the plate. Pow! The door snapped shut with a force that lifted the trap an inch and scared some sparrows that were scratching in the nearby gravel.

After I recovered from my shock and wonder, I called the SPCA and cancelled the appointment. I took the trap inside and tested it again several times. Why had it not fired when Ammie stood on it while gobbling down her morning meal? Maybe she'd not stepped on the metal plate but stretched her neck so she could reach the food. But, no, I'd watched her step onto it and stand there while she wolfed down her chow. Were the cat gods watching over her?

Jon Michael Miller

Eleven

Next morning I tried again. Same result. She entered the device, stepped on the plate, devoured her food and casually strolled away. Another cancelled appointment. The receptionist at the SPCA recommended calling in a professional.

The Five O'clockers were now on my case. Everyone knew the urgency of the situation due to Tux's hanging about. But I was wondering if somehow I were being punished, or interfered with, by some divinity intent on teaching me a lesson about the evil of interfering with the natural world. Once again, Melville's whaling masterpiece came to mind.

You know, some people believe that God watches everything we do, and these people claim that God's vision is not exclusively focused only on Believers. They even have faith – well, here's a scenario: Your alarm clock fails to go off and your lateness allowed you to avoid a fatal crash that happened at the precise point an accident occurred when you'd have been there if the alarm had worked. God was protecting you. Here's another – you'd just the day before had a towel rack fastened next to your tub, and you slipped badly and saved yourself by grasping the very rack that had been added, thus protecting you from a shattered pelvis. Well, you know many of these mysterious happenings, I'm sure.

Maybe God was teaching me a moral lesson. Or merely saving one of his wild creatures. My quandary, however, whatever its source, caused me to back off the trapping option. And as I tarried, Ammie's belly grew. I suggested that someone else try the trap, but there were no takers. It was clear to everyone that the responsibility was entirely mine.

"You started this whole bizarre situation," someone said.

Then we had a run of terrible weather. Hurricane Irma was on its way up the spine of the Florida peninsula. That looming catastrophe became everyone's concern. People hoarded bottled water. Spam, beef jerky and dried apricots sold out. Storm shutters were closed, windows boarded up, evacuation orders issued. We were in for a direct Category Five hit.

Of course, I worried about my wife's and two cats' safety, but also on my mind was poor Ammie, out and about in the rising turmoil. Certainly, she'd survived storms before, knew where the dry spots were, but this was different. Alas, however, I was helpless – took food out, but she was, essentially, on her own.

St. Pete lucked out, though, Irma taking a slight turn toward the east and sparing us her direct fury. It was a long night, wind howling, trees thrashing, sheets of rain rattling our doors and windows, and finally, toward morning, settling to a relatively strong but usual thunderstorm. When the light of dawn appeared, I slipped out to see the damage, and there was Ammie, huddled in a walkway corner where our building takes a hard right turn.

Snowball had been safely taken in by Jocelyn, but Ammie would never venture indoors, was satisfied and brave enough to endure the storm in her own environment. So there she was, quaking in a concrete corner as the wind continued to howl and rain poured down. But amazingly enough, her little corner was dry.

Thus, in spite of downed palm trees and broken branches from the live oaks and debris everywhere, life slowly returned to normal. But trapping Ammie took a back place in my priorities —except for one startling occurrence. Part of my routine was to rise about

six, clean the cat box and take out the trash.
But this particular morning, when I opened
the door – there was Ammie. She had somehow managed to locate my unit on the second
floor in the center of the building. She was
waiting for me!

Beneath my shock somewhere, a smile
arose. As I walked toward the trash chute, she
rubbed fleetingly against my ankles and slip-
pers. My smile grew into a laugh, until, at last
I leaned down for a pet and received one of
her ferocious hisses. She backed off, but when
I straightened up and began strolling, she was
rubbing against my calves again. Inside, I put
her food in her dish, and when I went back
out she'd been waiting for me, and followed,
meowing, to the usual feeding spot, now
strewn with leaves and twigs. Feverishly, she
gulped down her food.

The world slowly recovering from nature's fury and Ammie growing ever fatter,

she continued her charming morning visits to my door. Then, one morning she wasn't there. Nor was she at the feeding spot. I guessed where she was, though. I'd followed her once, remember? To over on the other side of the bank where she'd taken up in a barred culvert at the end of a drainage ditch near busy 54th Avenue. This morning the ditch was still filled with the hurricane runoff, allowing only a tiny, dry passageway down the steep bank to the culvert.

After calling Ammie's name and setting the dish at the top of the dry pathway, I backed off into the parking lot and waited. Then I saw Ammie's little face at the bars of the culvert. She looked around and saw me up the bank. I cooed at her and backed farther off. Slowly, cautiously, she ventured out of the culvert and up the bank to the food. She ate ravenously and returned to the culvert. She was no longer fat.

For the next ten days or so I carried her food to the drainpipe, as did Jocelyn in the evenings. But I knew I had a problem on my hands. Sooner or later, she would bring her kits to the usual feeding area. And, sure enough, one morning I opened my door and there she was, waiting on the walkway. As I carried the trash to the chute, she rubbed my legs and meowed. I took her morning meal to the usual area and heard some meek meowing from a patch of quackgrass. Ammie ate quickly and joined her offspring in the weeds.

Jon Michael Miller

Twelve

During all this time, of course, daily reports were provided to the Five O'clockers. Talk had turned from bunions and COPD, to Ammie's recent antics.

"Something has to be done," Mitch, the Mercedes owner, observed.

"Yes," Dorothy said. "We must handle the situation responsibly."

"Oh, I bet those kittens are so cute," Nan said.

"I wonder how many," Pam added.

"We never had cats," Jan jumped in, wearing a pair of her glitzy Zumba tights. "We had all kinds of animals, though. My second husband had three boys, and I had two, so we had five altogether. Great God Almighty! Five boys and all kinds of animals, and even those boys acted like animals always running around

the house playing football and wrastling, and
we had two dogs, five hamsters, parakeets,
rabbits – you name it, all kinds of animals running around. I wouldn't allow any iguanas
though. God bless America! My first husband
was in public relations, and my second was a
designer, and I was in hair care, worked in a
salon. Oh, my God, you should hear the stories, and my third husband's niece is in the
military, well, her husband is a helicopter pilot
but he wants to fly jets, so he's gonna have to
go to Alabama for training, and they gotta sell
their house, ha ha, Oh, my God! They call me
every day, actually I'm on the phone all hours
because I have five boys, and their wives and
kids, my grandkids. My granddaughter plays
soccer for her school, and runs track and has
the cutest little long-hair Chihuahua you ever
saw, but that dog is shy, scared of its own
shadow, so you see, I love animals, but I can't
have a cat cause I don't like them, and –"

"But," Mitch said again, "something has to be done."

"Well," I answered, as if thinking out loud, "the kittens won't be a problem because when they're weaned and friendly toward us, we can just pick them up and take them to Animal Services and they'll put them up for adoption."

"But as they're growing," Pam said, "some idiotic people around here are threatening to shoot them."

"Yeah," I replied. "The guy with the van. And the one who rides his bike around and thinks cats are a scourge."

"Well," Nan said, "I don't wanna name names, but I heard he has a gun. And guns are so easy to get. You can just go downtown and buy them right on the street. But yesterday Ammie ran out from under the van and almost attacked Ruth Tilton's Pekingese."

"And Snowball out there running around, leaving footprints on people's cars," Pam added. We love the cats, but...."

"Yeah," Mitch added, "it'll be a couple weeks for the kittens, but even then, what about Ammie?"

He had a point. They all had points. The other snowball I'd started was now rolling downhill becoming an avalanche.

So I revisited the trap I'd bought, still couldn't figure out why it wasn't working. I thought if I could get the cat clan used to me sitting next to it with food inside, I could manually close the door. So I started this plan.

Still mainly dependent on momma for nourishment, the four kittens were also beginning to eat from the dishes. So I placed the trap nearby and sat next to it with food inside. And in a day or two they all, including momma, began going in to eat. They went in and out, and even played by climbing on top of it, with me sitting there quietly biding my time.

I knew the main problem was Ammie. That if I caught her, took her in for surgery and brought her back in a day, we could at least tell the cat-haters that she wouldn't be creating a feral colony in one of our stairwells. Maybe we could even domesticate her, though that was highly doubtful. Although she greeted me every morning by prancing around joyously and rubbing my ankles, there was no way I could touch her. I tried nipping the tip of her tail, and she gave me her harrowing hiss that said, "No f-ing way."

With pressure from the detractors, I finally set the trap to at least get Ammie, the kittens now feeding mostly from the dishes. I knew I could take her to the emergency vet and they would do the surgery and release her back to me. Then the growing trustful kittens could be caught by hand and found homes.

The trap was set for me to spring manually. I didn't know what was wrong with the damn contraption. I sat quietly beside it with a dish of Fancy Feast at the closed end, just behind the metal plate. When Ammie was busy eating, I intended to press the plate hard enough to snap the front door closed. So, Ammie approached, but followed by one of the more adventurous kits. Ammie stepped onto the plate and began eating, but then the kitten went in too.

The both of them in there made me pause to consider the ramifications of catching them together. It would be dangerous for the kitten. But when the baby stepped onto the plate along with momma, the slightly added weight snapped the trap. I jumped with shock.

The closing of the cage was violent. Then came howling and cage-rattling from Ammie wanting to escape. In amazement, the

Five O'clockers stopped discussing Nan's bronchitis medication and looked down from the second floor. The howling in the trap went on. When I reached for the carry-handle of the cage, Ammie growled, hissed and tried to attack my hand. I'd brought a beach towel to cover the cage, knowing darkness would be less stressful. The towel draped over the device, I lifted it and headed toward my car.

That was when I heard the scream — yes, a scream I shall never forget. It was a cry, almost human, an extended shriek — blood-curdling — a wail of capture, the shock of betrayal, of horribly misplaced trust, of impending death. Just one long scream for help. Then, the silence of surrender.

I unlocked my trunk and set the trap inside. I was breathing hard, but not from the effort of carrying the cage. No, I was breathless from the emotion of all my good intentions coming down to one horrifying, hopeless scream, almost human, into the universe.

With the cage now in the closed trunk, I caught by breath. The emergency pet hospital didn't open until six, half an hour away. I went upstairs and ignored the quiet congratulations of the Five O'clockers.

"Would you like me to come with you?" Mitch asked.

It was a kind request for moral support from a very kind man. Not that he was needed for anything other than his sense of my conflicted feelings. I immediately accepted his offer of company. The mood of everyone there was somber. I went inside, sat down a moment with my eyes closed, then drank some cold water. I told myself that this was for the best, that we'd soon have Ammie and the kitten back to at least assuage our critics by having put an end to Ammie's reproductive cycle, as if she would be happily relieved from the tribulations of motherhood.

Well, maybe it would be a liberation if it hadn't been the ultimate purpose of her existence. And I couldn't get that long, tortured scream out of my brain.

Jon Michael Miller

Thirteen

On the way with Mitch to the pet hospital I was expecting a lot of thumping and yowling from the trunk. But there was only an eerie and heartbreaking silence all the way, even as I carried the cage into the facility. I sensed momma and child huddling in abject terror. The attendant assured us that the mom and kit would be taken care of at the main center of Animal Services the next morning. I signed some papers, and she took the cage to the back room. Soon, she returned.

"No way can I get them out of the trap," she said. "That momma cat is sure not happy. I'll have to wait for the guys in the truck tomorrow morning. Then you can contact the main office for the next steps. You can come back tomorrow for the trap and towel."

"You won't put them down," I said.

"No, we wouldn't do that."

"We want to release them back," I said.

"I understand."

Mitch and I didn't talk much on the twenty-minute drive home. "You did the right thing," was all he said, no doubt feeling my mood.

After a sleepless night trying to convince myself that my intentions had been, and still were, good, and that as Mitch had assured me, I'd done the right thing, and after being similarly assured by my wife, I rose for the morning feeding.

The remaining three kittens had retreated to under the van, surely wondering where their mother had gone. I put the dishes close to a front tire and backed off. They were hesitant to come out to eat. But eventually hunger drew them into the light. They first poked their little noses out, took a step, backed off, came out farther. At last the bravest of them ventured to the dish, soon to be followed by the other two. The moment the food was gone, they were back under the vehicle. At least, their mother would be back soon.

Jocelyn was a constant presence during all this activity, wringing her hands, worry on her face as I explained the situation with Animal Services.

"When can I pick them up?" she asked.

"I'll find out this evening when I get the trap," I answered.

But when I did go back, I got some amazing news.

"Somehow," the attendant said, "this morning when the men came for their usual pickup, the two cats got out."

"Huh? What's that?"

"Yeah, they got out."

"Where are they? Somewhere in the neighborhood?"

"No, not outside. They're still in the back, somewhere. The men will be here again tomorrow to catch them. There's a lot of stuff back there, boxes, supplies. They're somewhere. But we have your trap for you."

"But, they'll be okay, won't they?"

"They're very wild, sir. But we'll see what we can do. You can call Animal Services tomorrow, I'd say in the afternoon. I'm sure we'll get the situation under control by then."

Stunned, I drove back and told Jocelyn this amazing tale.

"They escaped?" she said, wide-eyed.

"Yeah, and they couldn't catch them, with all the stuff stored there."

"I'm gonna drive up to Animal Services first thing," she said. "I'm gonna make sure we get them back."

"Of course you will. But isn't that just like Ammie, though?" I said, suddenly respecting her wildness, her resolute fight for her freedom.

About three next afternoon, my phone rang – Jocelyn, just back from the headquarters of Animal Services. She was crying, stammering.

"We're not getting Ammie back," she said through her sobs. "They say she's too wild, a danger, unfit for adoption. I raised all kinds of hell, but they won't listen."

"What about the kitten?"

"Oh, they say they'll try to tame it down, but they doubt it. Oh, I'm so mad. I put up quite a fuss. They threatened to call the cops if I didn't leave."

They never did release the kitten. Ammie and her babe were gone. It left me with a sick, sad feeling inside. And a lot of guilt.

"Ammie is in a better place," Pam said.

"Kitty Heaven," Nan echoed.

"Too bad we couldn't get her to some place other than Animal Services," Mitch added.

"You did the right thing," Dorothy assured me.

"My God!" Jan said. "I had many pets that died, I buried two husbands, that's life, just the way it is, nothin' we can do about it, we just go on, make the best of things. Pets were always dying around our place, you get them when they're so little and cute, and take care of them, and they grow up and die, God bless America! God has a plan for everything, so just don't think about it, just go on step after step and get the most out of it, and then we die and go on to be with our maker, that's the way I look at things. What are ya gonna do? That cat was wild, and it was hiding under cars and then attacking dogs going by with their owners, and people were getting pissed off, pardon my French, Oh, my God! And something had to happen or we'd have cats coming out our galoshes, so you took care of the damn thing, and then things got out of hand and you hadda do what you hadda do, and that's the end of it, no use crying over spilt milk, what I always say. Hey, I buried two husbands, one damn cat is nothing to that, may God rest in peace and—"

"You did the right thing, Mike," Dorothy said with empathetic eyes. "And the kittens have homes, and we have Snowball. All's well that ends the best it can."

With that mangled Shakespeare quote lingering in my ears, I was at least determined to get the other three kits good homes. They were wandering around the van meowing for their momma. Carlos, the guy who'd tried to kidnap Snowball, managed to get one. It was felt that the responsibility might give him a stronger sense of community.

I took the other two kits in a carrier to a physical therapy facility next to the bank, and two of the workers there agreed to take them on the spot. So some good came of it all, I guess. Snowball is now comfortably ensconced in Jocelyn's domicile, resigned, it seems, to domesticate indoor living. And Tux doesn't come around anymore. So there are no cats and kittens scampering here and there to amuse the Five O'clock crowd.

Thus, we're all back to discussing our liver spots and deliberating about which restaurant serves the best crab cakes.

And me? Well, I've resolved to mind my own damn business and to allow Nature to mind its. And Ammie and her kitten? Gone to a better place? Kitty heaven? ... In my mind and in my heart, they're simply gone. And why? Because of me, that's why.

I knew then that my existential angst about what I did would be long in passing. And about that, at least, I have been right.

End

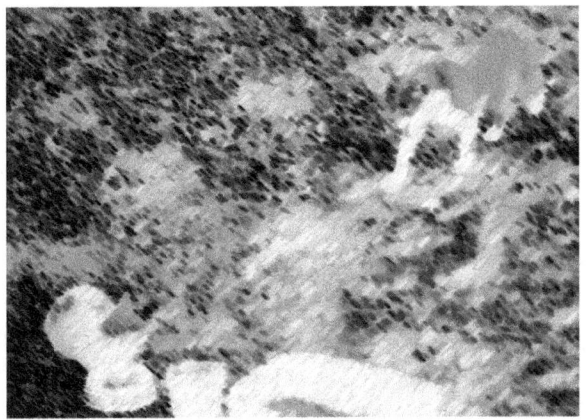

Ammie approaches Snowball at feeding time.

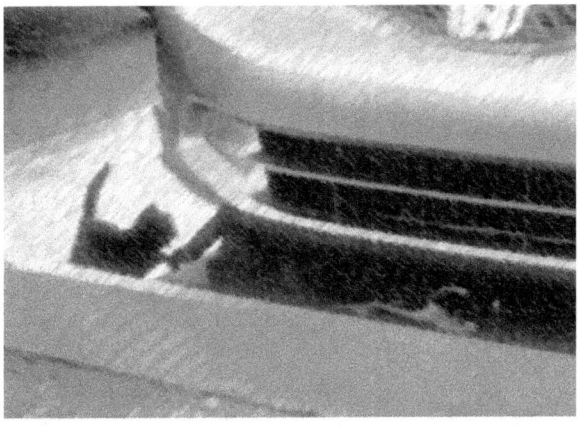

Snowball (under car) plays with brother.

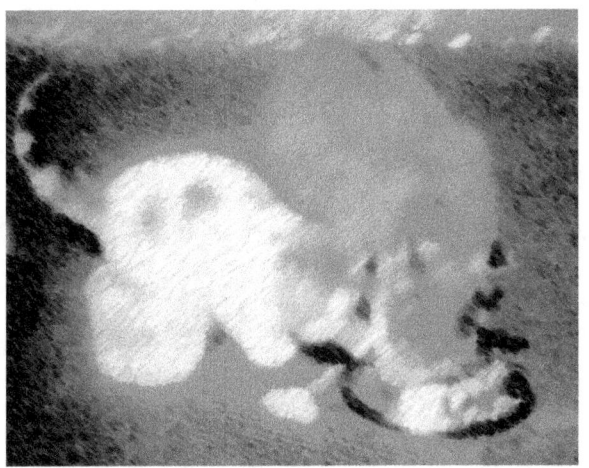

Mommy & daughter share Tuna Tenders.

Ammie & Snowball stroll to the dumpster.

Read Jon Michael Miller's other cat book:

JACKIE CHAN, the CAT

A Biography

Also of interest, a wry condo novel:

MURDER & MAYHEM IN

TROPIC GARDENS

Both available with his other writings at:

Amazon.com/author/jonmichaelmiller

Contact: mickymiller99@gmail.com

(Note: no "e" in "micky")